Cooking With Beans
and Pulses

With Foreword and
Star Recipes by
Rose Elliot

HOLLAND & BARRETT

Published exclusively for
Holland and Barrett, Aldwych House,
Madeira Road, West Byfleet,
Surrey KT14 6DA
by Thorsons Publishing Group Ltd,
Wellingborough, Northamptonshire

First published 1986

ISBN 0 7225 1332 1

Design, styling and photography by Paul Turner
and Sue Pressley, Stonecastle Graphics,
Tunbridge Wells, Kent

Printed in Italy

STAR RECIPES COURTESY
OF ROSE ELLIOT

Contents

Foreword

Beans and lentils are some of the most exciting, versatile and health-giving ingredients available. They can be made into delicious dishes which are packed with nourishment for the minimum cost. The renewed interest in these ancient foods is most encouraging, and I am delighted to write the foreword, and supply some recipes, for this book.

If you sometimes get the feeling that not a day passes without some food scientist finding out something unhealthy about one of your favourite foods, I've good news for you! With beans and pulses, the opposite seems to be the case, and there appears to be no end to the good things which are being discovered about these simple and ancient foods. One of the latest is that, in addition to the good quality protein, iron, calcium and B vitamins which they contain, beans and pulses are some of the richest known sources of soluble fibre, which helps to control blood-sugar and cholesterol levels, and to bring down high blood pressure.

Although the preparation of beans and pulses is very simple and straightforward, it involves techniques such as soaking and slow simmering, which, in this age of convenience foods, seem to be becoming lost arts! This is off-putting to some people. Yet all that is really required is a little forethought; the actual processes couldn't be easier, as this book explains. And once you've prepared your beans or lentils, there is wide scope for using them, as a glance through the recipes will show. The soaked and cooked beans can also be frozen in suitably-sized portions, and (though it's best to let them thaw for several hours at room temperature) they can be de-frozen under the hot tap for immediate use.

If you're new to bean and pulse cookery, try cooking them then adding them to a favourite vegetable stew; or make a meat casserole as usual, but replace a proportion of the meat with cooked beans: red kidney beans or butter beans are especially good in this kind of dish. In either case, you'll increase the fibre content of the dish and decrease the amount of saturated fat, thus making a healthier but just as tasty result. The dish will also be just as good nutritionally; you can use beans or lentils freely as meat and fish replacements and the results will only be beneficial.

One problem which many people raise is the question of indigestibility, and there's no doubt that some people do seem to have more sensitive digestive systems than others. If you're one of the sensitive ones, start by having small quantities, and gradually increase as your tolerance builds up. Prepare your pulses carefully, washing them well after soaking, then cooking them in fresh water. Don't assume that because you find one variety indigestible, this will apply to them all. Experiment with different types; the little red-brown adzuki beans are said by macrobiotic experts to be the most digestible. Some people say that the smaller the bean, the more digestible, and seem to get on specially well with split red lentils, yet I've met other people who find these the worst, so it does seem to be very much an individual matter. You may also find that sprouting your beans before use destroys the substance that upsets you; follow the instructions given in this book, and use the beans after a day or so, once the little shoots begin to appear. They can be used raw in salads, or forked into cooked rice, or cooked in water until tender, then made into burgers, soups, loaves and so on in the usual way.

One of the pleasures of cooking with beans and pulses, apart from their beautiful colours and shapes, is their versatility. I can think of no other ingredient which is equally at home in such a wide range of recipes, including soups and dips, salads and main courses; which can be eaten both cooked and sprouted; which can be made into a flour, a milk and a curd; and which is so nourishing, health-giving and cheap, to boot! Beans and pulses are indeed wonder foods, so, if they're new to you, do give them a try — you've a feast of discovery before you! And if you've already tried them, do look at some of the more unusual ones, or experiment with different ways of preparing them. The scope is wide, the possibilities exciting, and the effect on your health and your budget extremely rewarding. Happy cooking!

Boost Your Diet with Beans and Pulses

Pulses are dried peas, beans and lentils which belong to the *leguminosae* family and they make a splendid addition to the diet. Indeed, nutritionally, gastronomically and economically, they deserve to play a major part, and often do for vegetarians and especially vegans. Soya beans, for example, offer more protein than meat, eggs or cheese and many other beans boast a similar food value. They are also low in available carbohydrate and fat with a calorific value of just 26 calories per 25g (1 oz) when cooked. All beans are a splendid source of vegetable fibre, providing roughage essential for a healthy digestive system — they are also rich in iron, potassium, calcium and phosphorus and the B group vitamins, riboflavin and niacin.

Contrary to previous beliefs, all the beans and grains contain all the amino acids but, from the body's point of view, they are rather unbalanced and some will tend to be wasted unless they are combined with additional factors from other 'complementary' proteins. This is why it is a good idea nutritionally to combine beans with another type of protein such as that from dairy products (milk, cheese, yoghurt and eggs) or cereal, seed and nut products (rice, wheat, bread, pasta, nuts, sesame and sesame cream — tahini — sunflower and pumpkin seeds). This is almost second nature, however, as some popular and well-loved dishes round the world show, from that great British standby, beans on toast, to vast numbers of bean and rice combinations, chick pea *hummus* with bread, lentil soup with croûtons. The different types of protein serve to complement each other and give full nutritional value.

The aim of this book is to answer most of your questions about beans and pulses and offer a wide range of tempting recipes which will help to introduce them to your dining table or expand your repertoire with more adventurous use.

Star recipes in each section represent those which are a little 'extra-special'.

Soaking and Cooking for Best Results

Most peas and beans are improved by soaking before cooking. This shortens subsequent cooking time and helps to reduce problems with possible indigestibility and flatulence experienced by a few people by removing some of the ogliosaccharides. It also helps some types of beans to keep their shape.

Those who have trouble digesting them prefer to drain soaked beans before cooking, whilst others use the soaking water because it contains vitamins and minerals.

Long Soak

This is the time-honoured method for soaking beans. Pick over beans, removing damaged ones and grit and rinse well under cold running water. Cover beans with cold water (about 2L for 450g/1 lb) and leave to stand for 6-8 hours or overnight in a cool place then drain, rinse and drain again before cooking. Don't leave them to stand for too long, however, in case they begin to germinate. As a general guide, the harder the bean, the more it will benefit from longer soaking so this method is advisable for soya beans, chick peas and butter beans especially, helping them to cook more easily.

Short Soak

Perhaps fortunately, a much speedier method can be successfully employed for most of the slightly softer beans and peas, including red kidney, borlotti, black eye, etc. Pick over the beans and rinse, then cover with boiling water and leave for 10 minutes. If time permits, drain and repeat, otherwise drain, rinse and cook. Alternatively, they can be left to soak in hot water for about an hour. Lentils and split peas do not need to be soaked at all but it does speed up their cooking time.

The average length of time each type of bean requires to cook is given in the section describing the individual varieties but this does tend to vary with the age of the bean, etc. If you have a large quantity of beans from the same batch, it is a good idea to make a note of the time taken to cook the first batch for future reference. When soaked and cooked, beans roughly double in weight and 225g (8 oz) dry weight is usually sufficient for a main meal for four people, halving this for a first course.

Do not season or add salt to beans when cooking as this tends to toughen the skins. Remember that beans have flavours of their own which should be complemented and not drowned by flavourings.

Pressure Cooking

A quick method for cooking some of the less hard beans such as red kidney, borlotti and black eye, is to rinse and pick over in the usual way, cover with boiling water and leave them to soak for 10 minutes. Then drain, rinse and cook for about 30 minutes. Cooking at 15 lbs pressure usually reduces cooking time to between half and one-third but this does vary from batch to batch so it might be advisable to check close to the end of cooking time to avoid reducing beans to a mushy end! Split red lentils and split peas can tend to foam up and clog the valve when they come to the boil — adding a little fat or oil (about 2 tbsp) should prevent this. Pressure cooking is very helpful in speeding up the cooking of soya beans. After 30-40 minutes, they should be sufficiently softened to add to casseroles to cook with the other ingredients.

Dry Grinding

Another way to speed up meal-making is to dry-grind pulses in an electric coffee grinder. The pulses are washed and picked over as usual then well-dried on kitchen paper to make sure there is no remaining moisture. Grind a little at a time — the finer the powder, the quicker the cooking. The powder will keep for about a week in a dry screw-top jar. It can be used for pâtés, spreads, rissoles, loaves, burgers, or for soups, casseroles and stews. For the latter, mix 2-3 tbsp of the ground pulses with a cupful of hot stock or cooking liquid, then add to the rest of the ingredients, stirring often.

For pâtés, burgers, etc, gently cook the ground pulses in a little water until very thick, allow to cool, then mix with the other ingredients.

Think Ahead — Save Time and Effort!

Cook more than you need for various dishes. Cooked beans will keep well for up to four days in the fridge and will be on hand to add to salads or to any hot dish at the last minute. They can be used as a basis or filling and nutritious addition to soups or processed into a rapid starter or snack, or sandwich filling.

Beans and pulses are so versatile and full of flavour that you will soon make them part of many of the family's meals and wonder how you managed without them.

A-Z of Popular Pulses

Adzuki Beans

(Phaseolus angularis)

(also called aduki beans)

Description
Tiny, darkish-red beans, pointed at one end. Rich in protein.

Flavour and texture
Soft, nutty, slightly sweet taste.

Uses
Because of their sweet taste, adzuki beans are often cooked with rice, their bright colour tinting the rice pink, or they can be used in sweet dishes, soups and salads. They are especially good in vegetable stews. Be careful not to overspice them and spoil their delicate flavour. They can also be made into flour. In most dishes, the larger red beans may be substituted.

Average cooking time: 1-1½ hours.

Black Beans

(Phaseolus vulgaris)

Description

A member of the kidney bean family, these large (1.5cm, ½ inch long) shiny black beans are white inside, making a nice contrast, and are much used in Caribbean cookery.

Flavour and texture

Black beans share a tasty and succulent mealy texture with all kidney beans and have a rich, slightly sweet taste.

Uses

Black beans retain their colour when cooked so they make an attractive contrast to other beans when used in salads and casseroles. They can be substituted for red kidney beans in any recipe and are also widely used to produce bean sprouts.

Average cooking time: 1-1½ hours.

Black-eyed Beans

(Vigna unguiculata)

(also called black-eyed peas or cow peas)

Description
Black-eyed beans are a variety of cow pea. They are creamy-coloured, kidney-shaped and smaller than black beans with a distinctive black spot or 'eye' which gives them their name, and a roughish skin.

Flavour and texture
Pleasant, slightly sweet flavour with a succulent texture.

Uses
Black-eyed beans turn a faint pink with smooth skins when cooked and can be used as a substitute for haricot and butter beans if these are indigestible. Their flavour is complemented by cinnamon.

Average cooking time: 35-45 minutes.

Borlotti Beans

(Phaseolus vulgaris)

(also called borletti, salugia, crab-eye and rose cocoa beans)

Description
Another member of the kidney bean family, kidney-shaped and ranging in colour from a pale creamy pink (the best ones) to a deep brownish pink, and speckled.

Flavour and texture
Tender, moist texture with a pleasant sweetish flavour.

Uses
Borlotti beans can be used in any recipe instead of kidney or haricot beans, including soups, salads, main dishes and casseroles.

Average cooking time: 1 hour.

British Field Beans

(term includes tic and daffa beans)

Description
Roundish in shape, with a shiny brown skin similar to sweet chestnuts, these grow readily in gardens and allotments.

Flavour and texture
Tasty, with a slightly earthy flavour, and skins tend to be a little tough.

Uses
British Field Beans turn a darker brown when cooked and because of their skins are usually recommended for soups which can be liquidized and sieved or put through a vegetable mill after cooking and before adding to other ingredients. These beans are also very good for dips and burgers They can also be dry ground to overcome the skin problem.

Average cooking time: 30-60 minutes.

Broad Beans

(Vicia faba)

Description
Large, flat and kidney-shaped, with a tough greyish-green or brownish skin.

Flavour and texture
Broad beans are tasty but are best with the skins removed before serving.

Uses
Good with chunky casseroles or, as with other field beans, these can be liquidized and sieved after cooking for soups, etc, put through a vegetable mill or dry ground to avoid the skin problem.

Average cooking time: 1½ hours.

Butter Beans

(Phaseolus lunatus)

Description
Well-known in Britain, this is a large, flattish kidney-shaped bean of a creamy-white colour which becomes slightly translucent when cooked.

Flavour and texture
Pleasantly mealy when properly cooked, with a strong savoury taste which goes well with thick brown sauces.

Uses
Butter beans can be served as a vegetable or as a salad ingredient. They are also very good in curries, casseroles, pies and hot-pots, pâtés and spreads. They absorb flavours very well. All recipes for red beans are suitable for white beans.

Average cooking time: 45-60 minutes.

Cannellini Beans

(Phaseolus vulgaris)

(also called Fazolia beans)

Description
A variety of haricot or kidney bean, popular in Italy, which resembles small white kidney beans.

Flavour and texture
Pleasant and mealy.

Uses
Good for pâtés and spreads and they can also be used in any recipe specifying ordinary white haricot beans with which they contrast well, or butter beans or red kidney beans.

Average cooking time: 1-1½ hours.

Chick Peas

(Cicer arietinum)

(also called by their Spanish name of garbanzo or garbanzo pea, or Bengal gram — the Indian word meaning pulse or legume)

Description
Chick peas resemble small roundish dry hazelnuts and are a creamy golden-brown in colour, high in protein and very nutritious.

Flavour and texture
Chick peas have a distinctive, delicious and nutty flavour with an especially appetizing aroma.

Uses
They keep their shape well when cooked and are used in many recipes from the Middle East, India and Mexico. They are often used in spreads and pâtés like the Greek *Hummus*. They are also very good in salads, casseroles, dips and croquettes.

Average cooking time: 1-2 hours.

Continental Lentils

(Lens esculenta)

(also called 'green lentils' or 'brown lentils')

Description
These can, in fact, be grey, green, yellow or reddish-brown and are large, flat and lens-shaped.

Flavour and texture
Continental lentils retain their shape when cooked and are strong and tasty with a slightly earthy flavour.

Uses
They make a useful textural addition to a variety of bean dishes such as stews and casseroles. They also make good meatless burgers and are delicious spiced and served with warm wholewheat bread.

Average cooking time: Soaked — 25-30 minutes; unsoaked — 1-1½ hours.

Flageolet Beans

(Phaseolus vulgaris)

Description
Long and slim with a delicate pale green colour.

Flavour and texture
As these are really young haricot beans, they have a tender texture and a delicate, subtle flavour.

Uses
Although some of their colour disappears during cooking, flageolets still make an attractive addition to salads or bean mixtures and make a very delicately flavoured purée or a pretty pale green soup. They can also be used in the same way as dried white haricot beans.

Average cooking time: 30-60 minutes.

Ful Medames

(Lathyrus sativus)

Description
Smallish, dark brown beans with a rather tough outer skin.

Flavour and texture
Pleasant, 'earthy' flavour.

Uses
Ful Medames are very popular in the Middle East where they are served at any mealtime including breakfast, often flavoured with garlic, olive oil and lemon juice.

Average cooking time: 1 hour.

Haricot Beans

(Phaseolus vulgaris)

(also called white haricots, navy beans and Great Northern beans)

Description
This familiar variety of kidney bean is small, oval and creamy-white and perhaps best known in Britain in their popular guise of 'baked beans'.

Flavour
Delicious when properly cooked, with a fine delicate flavour so avoid using with strong spices or herbs which will mask it. Nutmeg, parsley and cider all complement the flavour of these beans well.

Uses
Haricot beans are very versatile and useful, popular in stews and casseroles, but they can be prepared in a number of delicious ways.

Average cooking time: 1-1½ hours (2 hours soaking time in cold water is usually enough for these, otherwise they may begin to ferment and spoil their flavour and digestibility).

Lima Beans

(Phaseolus limensis)

Description
Similar in appearance to butter beans but smaller.

Flavour
Lima beans have a deliciously sweet flavour because of their high sugar content.

Uses
As for butter beans, these can be served as a vegetable or as a salad ingredient and in curries, casseroles, pies, hot-pots, pâtés and spreads.

Average cooking time: 45-60 minutes.

Mung Beans

(Phaseolus aureus)

Description
These are small, round and mossy-green in colour.

Flavour and texture
Sweetish, with a soft, slightly creamy texture.

Uses
Mung beans are perhaps best known in this country in their sprouted form as 'bean sprouts', but they can also be cooked in a relatively short time and used in any suitable savoury dish.

Average cooking time: Soaked — 25-30 minutes; unsoaked — 30-40 minutes. Sprouted beans only need to be cooked for 1-2 minutes so add them at the end of cooking time.

Peas

(Pisum sativum)

Description
Dried peas resemble pale wizened fresh peas and can be green or yellow.

Flavour
Pleasantly sweet.

Uses
Familiar as 'mushy peas', these can also be made into purées or used as an ingredient of soups and stews.

Average cooking time: 45-60 minutes.

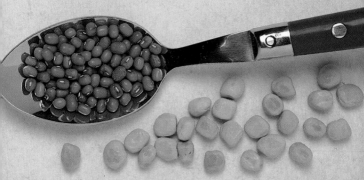

Pinto Beans

(Phaseolus vulgaris)

(also called zebra beans)

Description
Another variety of haricot bean, pinto beans are of medium size and resemble speckled borlotti beans.

Flavour
Tasty and savoury.

Uses
Pinto beans turn a pinky colour when cooked and make an attractive addition to dishes suitable for haricot beans.

Average cooking time: 1-1½ hours.

Red Kidney Beans

(Phaseolus vulgaris)

(also called Mexican or chilli beans)

Description
About 1.5cm (½ inch long), plump and kidney-shaped as their name indicates, with an attractive, glossy rich red colour.

Flavour and texture
Deliciously savoury but light flavour with a rather floury texture.

Uses
Well-known through their association with the Mexican dish Chilli Con Carne, red kidney beans turn maroon when cooked and make a colourful addition to many other dishes including soups, salads and casseroles.

Average cooking time: 1-1¼ hours.

Soya Beans

(Glycine max)

Description
Small, round and hard, about pea-sized and usually ivory-coloured or yellowish-brown, soya beans have the highest nutritional value of the pulses, are low in starch and the only ones to contain fats and all the essential amino acids necessary to make a complete protein. They are available whole or split.

Flavour and texture
Similar to young, fresh green peas and quite different to any other bean in flavour and texture when cooked, being firm and a little oily.

Uses
After soaking, soya beans can be added as they are to salads; cooked, they make a good ingredient for substantial main courses like goulash and hot-pot. A soft, yellow, protein-rich flour is also made from soya beans which can be used to make non-dairy milk and 'cheeses' such as bean curd (tofu).

Average cooking time: 1½-3 hours.

Split Peas

(Pisum sativum)

Description
Both green and yellow varieties are readily available in most supermarkets and health food shops. All split peas have had their outer skin removed.

Flavour and texture
Green split peas normally have a lighter and fresher flavour than the yellow type which can taste slightly musty, and both are usually cooked to a purée.

Uses
In puréed form they can be served as they are or made into pease pudding, loaves, croquettes, rissoles, soups and other savoury dishes or used as stuffings for vegetables.

Average cooking time: Soaked — 25-30 minutes; unsoaked — 45-60 minutes.

Split Red Lentils

(Lens esculenta)

(also called Egyptian lentils)

Description

Bright orangey-red split lentils are the most widely available in shops and supermarkets but they can also be found in green, yellow and brown.

Flavour and texture

With a pleasantly distinct savoury flavour that is stronger than that of many beans, these do not hold their shape when cooked, reducing to a soft mass.

Uses

Split lentils cook quickly to a light golden-beige purée so they are good for soups, croquettes, quiches and loaves or, with oil and vinegar, make a good salad. They blend very well with the flavour, colour and texture of other ingredients.

Average cooking time: Soaked — 15-20 minutes; unsoaked — 20-30 minutes.

Bean Bonuses

These are two very useful recipes which many people like to try making for themselves, which again illustrate the versatility of beans and pulses.

Home Made Bean Curd (Tofu)

225g (8 oz) soya flour
850ml (1½ pts) cold water
Juice of 2 lemons

Put soya flour and water into a good-sized saucepan and simmer gently for 5 minutes then stir in the lemon juice and ½ tsp sea salt. Leave mixture to cool — it will thicken up. Meanwhile, line a large sieve with a double layer of butter muslin or new, clean dishcloth material, leaving an overlap so that you can gather up the corners later. Set sieve over a bowl and pour the cooled soya mixture through the sieve, then gather up the piece of material and tie it. Suspend it over a bowl and leave it to drip for 8-12 hours. Once it has finished dripping you can firm it up by placing a plate and weight on top of it.

Keep the bean curd in a plastic container in the refrigerator. (These quantities make about 450g (1 lb) of bean curd.)

Tofu 'Whipped Cream'

225g (8 oz) tofu
2 tsp honey or raw sugar
Real vanilla extract or piece of vanilla pod

Drain water from tofu. Break into rough pieces and place in blender or food processor with honey or sugar and vanilla and whizz to a thick cream. Instead of vanilla you can use triple-distilled rose water, orange flower water or grated lemon or orange rind.

*Use firm tofu — home-made or shop bought. (The vacuum-packed type will not give such a thick effect.)

Sprouting Beans
and Pulses

Another bonus from beans and pulses from both the catering and nutritional point of view is the fact that they can be 'sprouted'. In this form they offer a very rich source of vitamins A and especially C, several of the B complex vitamins and they also contain a higher level of protein and amino acids than most vegetables. Some sprouts are also a good source of vitamins E, G, K and U. They can be used to increase the food value of a wide variety of dishes, especially salads to which they make a deliciously crunchy addition.

Many people have seen and bought bean sprouts from food stores and supermarkets or eaten them in Chinese-style meals. These are usually produced from the little round green Mung beans but any clean, good quality dried peas and beans can be used to produce 'sprouts' easily, economically and speedily in your own kitchen with just a glass jar, elastic band and a piece of muslin! Chick peas, adzuki beans and black beans make particularly good 'sprouts' and even whole lentils can be used although not, of course, split lentils or peas.

Specially-designed sprouting units are available but a jar will do just as well. Beans increase tremendously in volume when sprouted (at least sixfold) so don't attempt more than a tablespoon or two of dried peas or beans at a time. Wash the beans, cover them with cold water and leave to soak overnight. Next day, rinse them under cold running water and then put them in a large clean glass jar and cover the top of the jar with a piece of muslin or cheesecloth held in place by an elastic band. Keep the jar in a warm, dark and dry place or (if you are forgetful!) put it by the sink wrapped in brown paper to keep out the light, to remind you to rinse the beans two or three times a day by running cold water into the jar through the muslin. Swill it around to wash the beans and remove the toxins produced, then pour it out again without removing the muslin. If possible, leave the jar at an angle on the draining board to make sure that all the water drains away.

In an average of three to four days, the beans will be soft enough to eat and you can harvest them with deliciously crunchy sprouts attached for adding to salads, sandwiches, stir-fry vegetables and all manner of dishes. Steaming or stir-frying them for a few minutes preserves the vitamins in bean sprouts and is preferable to boiling if you are going to cook them. Raw, they will keep in the fridge for up to four days.

27

Soups and Starters

The contrast and variety of soups in colour, texture and flavours which can be made from the different types of beans and pulses is quite astonishing. They can make a light, delicately-coloured and attractive starter, especially sprinkled with suitable chopped fresh green herbs, swirled with a little thinned-down tofu, fromage blanc or quark low-fat soft cheese, or topped with crunchy croûtons or diced wholewheat toast. Or the more substantial ones, like Pistou, can make a comforting and warming lunch or supper for chilly days served with warm wholewheat bread or rolls and a little cheese, with fruit for dessert.

Although half-portions of most of the dishes in this book, particularly the salads, make excellent starters too, we have included several tasty suggestions in this section to fire your imagination.

Spicy Lentil Soup

225g (8 oz) yellow split peas or split red lentils
1 large onion
2 tbsp vegetable oil
1 garlic clove, crushed
1 tsp turmeric
1 tsp ground ginger
1 tsp curry powder
1 bay leaf
1L (1½ pts) water or vegetable stock
1 lemon
Sea salt; freshly ground black pepper

Cover peas or lentils with water. Soak and rinse. Peel and chop onion then sauté in oil in a large saucepan. Add garlic, spices and bay leaf and cook for a further 5 minutes. Add split peas or lentils and water or stock. Bring to boil, then simmer for 30 minutes. Remove bay leaf and liquidize soup (if a thicker version is preferred, add a cooked potato before liquidizing). Add juice of lemon to soup, then season to taste. Reheat before serving.

Approx. preparation and cooking time (not including soaking): 55 minutes.

Chick Pea Soup

225g (8 oz) chick peas
1 onion
2 carrots
50g (2 oz) butter
1 tbsp lemon juice
1 bay leaf
Sea salt; freshly ground black pepper
A few croûtons of fried bread

Soak chick peas in cold water for several hours or overnight, then drain and rinse. Put into saucepan with plenty of cold water and simmer gently until very tender (up to an hour or more). Drain chick peas, keeping liquid. Measure this and make up to 1.2L (2 pts) with some water or stock.

Peel and chop onion; scrape carrots and cut into dice. Melt half the butter in a large saucepan and fry onion and carrot for 5 minutes until golden brown. Stir often to prevent sticking then add chick peas, liquid, lemon juice and bay leaf and simmer soup gently until vegetables are tender — about 20 minutes. Take out bay leaf and liquidize soup. Put into clean saucepan, stir in remaining butter and season to taste. Serve topped with croûtons of fried bread.

Approx. preparation and cooking time (not including soaking): 1½ hours.

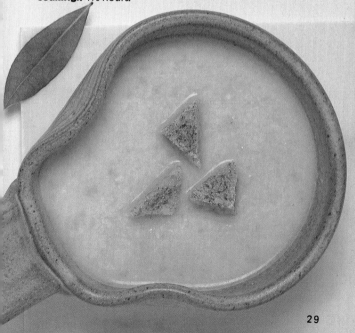

☆ Curried Rice and ☆ Chick Pea Ring

Serves 6
225g (8 oz) long grain brown rice
400ml (¾ pt) water
1 tsp sea salt
2 large onions, peeled and chopped
4 tbsp oil
4-6 tsp curry powder
2 crisp eating apples
2 bananas
Juice of ½ lemon
125g (4 oz) raisins
6-8 tbsp mayonnaise
225g (8 oz) chick peas, soaked, rinsed, cooked and drained

To serve:

1 small red pepper, de-seeded and sliced into thin rings
A little chopped parsley
½ bunch watercress

Wash and pick over rice, put into heavy-based saucepan with water and salt and bring to the boil. Then put lid on saucepan, reduce heat and leave rice to cook very gently for 45 minutes.

Fry onion in oil with curry powder for 10 minutes until soft but not browned; add half to the cooked rice. Peel and dice apples and bananas and toss in lemon juice. Cover raisins with a little boiling water and leave on one side for 10 minutes, then drain and add to rice with apple and banana. Season to taste. Press rice mixture into 1L (2 pt) ring mould (oiled) and leave to cool.

Stir remaining onion and curry into mayonnaise and add the chick peas; season. Turn rice ring out onto large serving dish and pile the chick pea mayonnaise into centre. Arrange red pepper rings around top of rice ring, sprinkle chick pea mayonnaise with chopped parsley. Then tuck some sprigs of fresh, bright green watercress around outside edge of ring. Serve with salad of bright orange grated carrots.

Approx. preparation and cooking time: 1½-2 hours.

Curried Lentil and Apple Soup

25g (1 oz) butter
1 onion, chopped
1 carrot, scraped and chopped
125g (4 oz) cooking apple, peeled and chopped
2 tsps curry powder
175g (6 oz) red lentils
1 bay leaf
850ml (1½ pts) water or stock
1 tbsp lemon juice
Sea salt; freshly ground black pepper

Heat butter in a large saucepan and fry onion, carrot, apple and curry powder for 10 minutes without browning. Then stir in lentils, bay leaf and stock or water. Bring to the boil, then simmer gently for 20-30 minutes until lentils and vegetables are cooked. Remove bay leaf. Liquidize soup, then return to saucepan, add lemon juice and season. Reheat or serve chilled with a little cream or natural yoghurt on top.

Approx. preparation and cooking time: 50 minutes.

Pea Soup with Mint

1 onion, chopped
25g (1 oz) butter
225g (8 oz) whole dried peas, soaked for 6-8 hours, drained and rinsed
1.7L (3 pts) water or unsalted stock
Small bunch mint, stalks removed
Sea salt; freshly ground black pepper; sugar
Lemon juice

Fry onion in butter, without browning, for 10 minutes then add peas and water. Bring to the boil, cover and simmer very gently for about 2 hours, until peas are soft. Add mint, then liquidize. Return to saucepan; season to taste with salt, pepper, a little sugar and lemon juice.

Approx. preparation and cooking time: 2 hours 20 minutes.

Yellow Split Pea Soup

225g (8 oz) yellow split peas
1.7L (3 pts) water
25g (1 oz) butter
1 large or 2 medium onions, peeled and finely chopped
1 garlic clove, peeled and crushed
25g (1 oz) wholewheat flour
Sea salt; freshly ground black pepper

Put split peas into saucepan with the water; let them simmer gently for 40-50 minutes until tender, then liquidize. Melt butter in rinsed-out saucepan and fry onion until golden, then stir in garlic and flour. Cook for a minute or two, then gradually pour in the split pea purée, stirring until mixture is smooth. Let soup simmer for 5-10 minutes to cook the flour, season to taste. The soup will be quite thick; thin with more liquid if preferred.

Remember to use a large saucepan to boil split peas as they bubble up when cooking. Adding a tablespoon or two of oil to the cooking water helps or, if the saucepan is not big enough, cook the peas using only 1.2L (2 pts) water, adding rest when liquidizing soup.

Approx. preparation and cooking time: 1 hour 10 minutes.

Bean and Carrot Soup

125g (4 oz) haricot beans, soaked, drained and rinsed
850ml (1½ pts) unsalted stock or water
1 large onion, peeled and sliced
1 stick of celery, sliced
2 large carrots, scraped and diced
Bouquet garni
25g (1 oz) butter
25g (1 oz) flour
275ml (½ pt) milk
Sea salt; freshly ground black pepper
Grated nutmeg
A little chopped parsley

Put beans in a large saucepan with stock or water and simmer gently for 45 minutes, then add onion, celery, carrots and bouquet garni. Cook for another 30 minutes or so until beans and vegetables are tender. Remove bouquet garni and sieve or liquidize soup.

Melt butter in a large clean saucepan and stir in flour; when it 'froths', remove saucepan from heat and stir in puréed soup. Put saucepan back on heat and stir soup until it has thickened. Leave to simmer gently for 10-15 minutes to cook the flour, then mix in milk and season soup with salt, pepper and grated nutmeg. Reheat soup but do not boil. Serve sprinkled with chopped parsley.

Approx. preparation and cooking time: 1 hour 40 minutes.

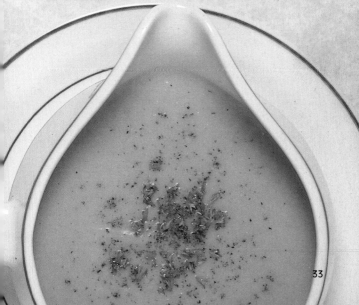

33

Flageolet Soup

125g (4 oz) flageolet beans
1 small onion
1 leek
25g (1 oz) butter
850ml (1½ pts) unsalted stock or water
2-4 tbsp double cream
1 tbsp chopped parsley
Sea salt; freshly ground black pepper
A little chopped fresh parsley

Soak, rinse and drain beans as usual. Peel and chop onion; well wash and shred leek, including as much of green part as possible, then cook gently together in the butter in a good-sized saucepan for about 10 minutes. Add beans to onion and leek, together with stock or water and simmer gently for about 1 hour, until beans are tender. Put soup into liquidizer goblet with cream and parsley and blend to a smooth creamy consistency. Season with salt and pepper. Reheat, but do not boil the soup and serve garnished with extra chopped parsley.

Approx. preparation and cooking time (not including soaking): 1 hour 25 minutes.

Cream of Butter Bean Soup

125g (4 oz) butter beans
1 large onion
1 medium-size potato
2 carrots
2 sticks celery
25g (1 oz) butter
850ml (1½ pts) water or unsalted stock
275ml (½ pt) milk
Bouquet garni
4-6 tbsp cream
Sea salt; freshly ground black pepper
Grated nutmeg
A few croûtons of fried bread

Soak butter beans, then drain and rinse. Peel and chop onion and potato; scrape and chop carrots; slice celery. Melt butter in a large saucepan and add vegetables. Sauté for 7-8 minutes without browning, then add butter beans, water or stock, milk and bouquet garni. Simmer gently with lid half on saucepan, for about 1¼ hours or until butter beans are tender. Remove herbs, then liquidize the soup, stir in cream and add salt, pepper and nutmeg to taste. Reheat soup but don't let it boil. Serve each bowl sprinkled with croûtons.

Approx. preparation and cooking time (not including soaking): 1 hour 40 minutes.

Chick Pea and Vegetable Mayonnaise

Serves 6-8 as a starter
175g (6 oz) chick peas
700g (1½ lbs) tender new vegetables (potatoes, carrots, French beans, shelled broad beans — cooked, drained and cooled)
400g (14 oz) can artichoke hearts, drained
1-2 large garlic cloves, crushed
6 rounded tbsp mayonnaise
6 rounded tbsp natural yoghurt
Sea salt; freshly ground black pepper
A little chopped fresh parsley

Cover chick peas with cold water and leave to soak for several hours, then drain and rinse and put into a saucepan with a good covering of water and simmer for 1-1½ hours until very tender. Drain chick peas thoroughly (cooking water makes good stock for soups and sauces).

Cut the cooked vegetables and artichoke hearts into chunky pieces and put in a bowl with the chick peas. Mix together garlic, mayonnaise and yoghurt, then add to vegetables in the bowl, turning them over gently until covered with the creamy mixture. Season with salt and pepper. Cool, then chill the salad. Serve it heaped on a serving dish or spoon salad onto crisp lettuce leaves on individual plates. Sprinkle top with chopped parsley for colour contrast and serve with warm soft wholewheat baps or pitta bread.

Approx. preparation and cooking time (not including soaking):

Pistou

450g (1 lb) green beans, sliced
450g (1 lb) mixed beans (adzuki, red kidney, black eye, haricots, etc, soaked and drained)
2 courgettes
4 carrots
2 tomatoes, peeled
2 potatoes
2 leeks
2.5L (5 pts) boiling water
Sea salt

Pistou sauce

2 garlic cloves, peeled
1 tsp dried basil
2 tbsp vegetable oil
Parmesan cheese

Cook the beans in water for about an hour until almost tender, drain and set aside. Wash and slice the courgettes, green beans and leeks. Dice the potatoes and carrots. Put all the vegetables into a saucepan with the boiling water and season with 1 tsp salt. Bring to the boil then reduce the heat and cover the pan. Cook for 10 minutes or until the vegetables are tender.

Meanwhile prepare the pistou sauce. In a mortar, pound together the garlic cloves with the basil to a smooth paste. Add the vegetable oil a little at a time. When well mixed, add 2 tbsp of the soup mixture, remove the soup from the heat and gradually add the pistou sauce. Serve sprinkled with the Parmesan cheese.

Approx. preparation and cooking time: 1 hour 10 minutes.

Dips and Spreads

A very versatile section! The recipes included here lend themselves as starters for a special meal; sandwich and pitta fillings, perhaps with the addition of finely-chopped salad vegetables — even the pâtés can be sliced thinly and used as sandwich fillings; super buffet party dishes; toppings for wholewheat snack biscuits, crispbreads or scones; or the softer ones make dips for crunchy vegetables such as celery, carrots, green and red pepper strips.

Remember that pulses to be used in chilled dishes should be cooked until very tender, but not mushy, otherwise they will tend to harden as they get colder. Mixtures should also be generously seasoned to make up for any loss of flavour during chilling and it pays to use a really good quality olive oil if the recipe calls for it, for the same reason.

Creamy Butter Bean Dip

100g (3-4 oz) butter beans, soaked and cooked or 1×425g (15 oz) can
1 tbsp olive oil
1 tsp wine vinegar
1 garlic clove, peeled and crushed
Sea salt; freshly ground black pepper

Drain butter beans, keeping liquid. Put all ingredients into liquidizer goblet with 2 tbsp of the liquid. Blend to a smooth purée, adding a little more liquid if necessary to make a thick but creamy consistency. Spoon into paté dish, fork top and decorate with a few black olives. Chill before serving with Sesame Toast.

Approx. preparation and cooking time: 5 minutes.

☆ Bean and Black Olive Pâté ☆ with Hardboiled Eggs

Serves 6
125g (4 oz) dried white beans (haricot, cannellini or butter beans, soaked and cooked) or 425g (15 oz) can butter beans
12 black olives, stoned
2 tbsp olive oil
2 tbsp lemon juice
Sea salt; freshly ground black pepper
Cayenne pepper
Crisp lettuce leaves
4 hardboiled eggs
Paprika pepper
Watercress
Lemon wedges

Drain beans, reserving liquid, and mash to a purée (needn't be too smooth). Stone olives then mash with a fork and add to the beans, together with oil and lemon juice. Stir in a little of the reserved liquid if needed to make a soft creamy mixture, the consistency of lightly whipped cream. Season with salt, pepper and a pinch of cayenne. Chill until required; it can be made several hours in advance.

Arrange 2 or 3 small crisp lettuce leaves in individual small bowls. Cut eggs into wedges and put them on top, dividing among the bowls. Spoon bean and olive mixture on top and sprinkle with a little paprika pepper. Decorate each bowl with a sprig or two of watercress and a wedge of lemon.

Approx. preparation and cooking time: 15 minutes.

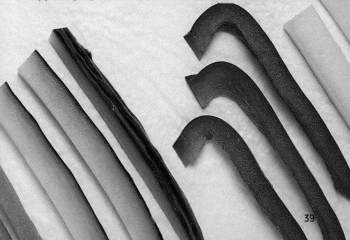

Sesame Toast

6 slices wholewheat bread
Butter or polyunsaturated margarine
Sesame seeds

Set oven to 400°F (200°C), gas mark 6. Cut crusts off bread and roll each slice with a rolling pin to flatten it a little. Spread bread with butter or margarine and sprinkle a good layer of sesame seeds on top, pressing them in with a knife. Cut bread into fingers and place on a baking sheet. Bake for 10-15 minutes, until crisp and golden brown. Serve at once with Creamy Butter Bean Dip.

Approx. preparation and cooking time: 20 minutes.

Lentil and Parsley Spread

125g (4 oz) red lentils
200ml (7 fl oz) water
50g (2 oz) butter
2 tbsp chopped parsley
Bunch spring onions, chopped
Pinch of chilli powder
1 tbsp lemon juice
Sea salt; freshly ground black pepper

Put lentils into a saucepan with the water and cook gently until lentils are tender and water absorbed — 20-25 minutes. Beat butter into lentils, together with parsley, spring onions, chilli, lemon juice and seasoning. Mix well to make a fairly creamy paste, adding a little water if necessary to achieve a spreading consistency.

Serve with toast or savoury biscuits. Also makes a good sandwich filling.

Approx. preparation and cooking time: 30 minutes.

Haricot Bean and Garlic Spread

125g (4 oz) haricot beans, cooked until tender, then cooled
25g (1 oz) soft butter
1 clove garlic, crushed
Few drops of lemon juice
Sea salt; freshly ground black pepper

Mash beans to a smooth paste with a fork, then gradually blend in butter, garlic and lemon juice. Season well with sea salt and freshly ground black pepper.

Serve with cocktail biscuits or wholewheat toast; also good as a sandwich spread.

Approx. preparation and cooking time: 10 minutes.

Variations

Haricot bean and parsley spread
Omit garlic from recipe and add 2 tbsp chopped fresh parsley.

Haricot bean and fresh herb spread
Instead of garlic add 2 tbsp chopped fresh herbs: parsley, chives, tarragon, mint, fennel, lovage, etc.

Haricot bean and olive spread
Omit garlic and use instead 4-6 black olives, stoned and mashed to a smooth paste.

Tofu and Avocado Whip

2 large avocados
275g (10 oz) tofu
Juice of ½ lemon
Freshly ground black pepper
Chives to garnish

Cut avocados in half and remove stones. Scoop out flesh and place in blender goblet. Add tofu and lemon juice and blend until smooth. Season with pepper. Turn into serving dish and smooth top then sprinkle with chopped chives. Serve with strips of raw vegetables.

Approx. preparation and cooking time: 10 minutes.

Continental Lentil and Mushroom Pâté

125g (4 oz) continental lentils
50g (2 oz) button mushrooms
1 clove garlic
40g (1½ oz) butter
1 tbsp chopped parsley
Sea salt; freshly ground black pepper
2-4 tsp lemon juice

Soak, drain, rinse and cook lentils in usual way until very tender and beginning to disintegrate. Drain off any extra liquid (can be used for gravy or soup as it is full of flavour and nourishment). Wipe mushrooms and chop fairly finely; crush garlic. Melt butter in a small saucepan and fry mushrooms and garlic for 2-3 minutes then remove from heat and mix in lentils and parsley. Season with salt, pepper and lemon juice. Chill before use. Serves 4-6 as a starter and makes a good sandwich filling.

Approx. preparation and cooking time (not including soaking): 30 minutes.

Hummus

Serves 8 as a starter
225g (8 oz) chick peas
8 tbsp olive oil
3 garlic cloves, peeled and crushed
4 tbsp lemon juice
4 tbsp sesame cream (*tahini*)
Sea salt
Paprika papper
Lemon wedges

Soak chick peas in plenty of cold water for several hours then drain and rinse. Put into a saucepan, cover with cold water and simmer for 1-1½ hours until tender, then drain, keeping the cooking water. Either pass chick peas through a vegetable mill then mix in half the olive oil and all the other ingredients, or use a liquidizer, putting chick peas in goblet with half the olive oil, garlic, lemon juice, sesame cream and some salt and blending to a smooth, fairly thick purée. You may need to add some cooking liquid to make a nice creamy consistency. Chill the *hummus* then serve on a flat dish with rest of olive oil spooned over top and a good sprinkling of paprika. Garnish with lemon wedges. If serving as a starter, however, it is easier to put individual portions on medium-size plates and top each with some olive oil and paprika. Serve with extra olive oil and plenty of soft wholewheat bread or pitta bread.

Approx. preparation and cooking time (not including soaking and chilling): 1 hour 35 minutes.

Bean Pâté

179g (6 oz) full medames beans, British field beans or continental (whole) lentils
2 tbsp olive oil
1 tbsp lemon juice
1 garlic clove, peeled and crushed
1 tbsp finely chopped parsley
Sea salt; freshly ground black pepper
Sugar
4 black olives
Fingers of hot wholewheat toast
Butter or polyunsaturated margarine

Cover beans well with boiling water and leave to soak for 4-5 hours (less if using lentils), then drain and rinse, put in a good-sized saucepan with plenty of cold water and simmer over gentle heat until tender (1¼-1½ hours for beans, 30-45 minutes for lentils). Drain beans or lentils, reserving liquid. Pass beans through a vegetable mill or mash lentils with a fork, then mix in olive oil, lemon juice, garlic, parsley, salt and pepper and, if necessary, enough of the reserved cooking liquid to make a thick creamy pâté. Taste mixture, adding a little sugar if required.

Spoon pâté into 4 small ramekin dishes, smooth surface and decorate each with an olive. Serve chilled with fingers of hot toast for people to spread first with butter or margarine, then pâté. Also good as a sandwich filling or spread on little biscuits.

Approx. preparation and cooking time (not including soaking): 1-1½ hours.

Salads and Dressings

Beans and pulses offer colourful and substantial salad ingredients — what can be more attractive, tasty or filling than a splendid Three Bean Salad, for example? Tender, young vegetables combined with a variety of different beans and pulses and coated with a simple vinaigrette dressing are almost always popular and a Mayonnaise and Yoghurt Dressing makes a delicious change. Bean salads can be used in small quantities as starters, in more substantial form with nutty brown rice or wholewheat bread as a main course lunch or supper, and any left over makes a splendid sandwich or pitta filling.

Dressings can make all the difference to a salad — a finishing touch with delicate flavourings which draw out deliciously the character of the beans and vegetables used.

☆ Three-bean Salad with ☆ Mustard Dressing

100g (3-4 oz) red kidney beans, soaked and cooked, or 1 × 425g (15 oz) can
225g (8 oz) frozen broad beans
225g (8 oz) French beans, frozen or fresh ones, trimmed
Sea salt
1 tbsp mild mustard (whole grain is good)
3 tbsp olive oil
1 tbsp wine vinegar
Freshly ground black pepper; summer savory
Fresh chopped parsley

Drain beans and put into a large bowl. Cook broad beans and French beans in a little fast-boiling water until just tender. Drain beans and add to bowl with red kidney beans. Mix dressing: put mustard into small bowl and stir in oil, vinegar, salt and pepper and a pinch or two of summer savory. Mix well, then pour into bowl with the beans, coating them thoroughly. If possible, let salad stand for 30 minutes or so to let flavours blend. Spoon salad into serving dish and sprinkle with chopped parsley. Serve with warm wholewheat bread or rolls, jacket potatoes or fresh salad.

Approx. preparation and cooking time: 25 minutes.

Mexican Salad

100g (3-4 oz) red kidney beans, soaked and cooked, or 1×425g (15 oz) can
1 large ripe avocado
1 garlic clove, peeled and crushed
1 tbsp olive oil
1 tsp wine vinegar
Sea salt; freshly ground black pepper; chilli powder
8 large crisp lettuce leaves
1 small onion, peeled and thinly sliced
4 firm tomatoes, sliced
1 small green or red pepper, de-seeded and thinly-sliced
125g (4 oz) grated cheese or 4 hardboiled eggs, sliced
Paprika pepper

Drain beans. Halve avocado, remove stone and skin. Put the avocado into a medium-sized bowl and mash with a fork. Add garlic, oil and vinegar to the avocado then season with salt, pepper and a pinch of chilli powder. Mix well to a creamy consistency.

Place two lettuce leaves on each plate. Spoon beans over lettuce and top with layers of onion, tomato, pepper and cheese or egg. Finish with a big dollop of the avocado cream and a good sprinkling of bright red paprika pepper. Serve at once.

Approx. preparation and cooking time: 15 minutes.

Rice and Bean Salad

125g (4 oz) red kidney beans (or other beans)
225g (8 oz) long grain brown rice
400ml (¾ pt) water
Sea salt
225g (8 oz) aubergine
1 clove garlic
1 large onion
2 tbsp oil
1 red pepper
125g (4 oz) mushrooms
225g (8 oz) canned tomatoes
Freshly ground black pepper
2 drops tabasco
A little chopped parsley

Soak beans, cook until tender then drain. Wash and pick over rice, put into saucepan with water and 1 tsp sea salt, bring to the boil and cook as usual over a very gentle heat with a lid on saucepan, until it is just tender and all the water has been absorbed — 45 minutes.

Wash the aubergine and cut into small pieces; sprinkle with sea salt and leave for 30 minutes so that the salt can draw out any bitter juices, then squeeze and rinse the aubergine and pat dry with kitchen paper. Crush garlic, peel and chop onion and fry in oil in a good-sized saucepan for 10 minutes, then add prepared aubergine and cook a minute or two longer while you de-seed and chop the pepper and wash and slice the mushrooms. Add pepper and mushrooms to saucepan with canned tomatoes and let everything cook for about 10 minutes more.

Using a fork, mix together cooked rice, vegetables and beans; season with salt, pepper and tabasco. Let salad get quite cold and serve sprinkled with chopped parsley.

Approx. preparation and cooking time: 1 hour.

Cannellini, Apple and Celery Salad

Serves 2-3

125g (4 oz) cannellini beans (or other white beans)

3 tbsp oil

1 tbsp lemon juice

Sea salt; freshly ground black pepper

1 celery heart

2 eating apples

2 tbsp raisins, washed and drained

Prepare and cook beans as usual; drain. Mix together oil, lemon juice, salt and pepper and add to beans, mixing gently. Wash and slice celery; wash apples and peel if the skin is tough, then cut into dice, discarding the cores. Add celery and apples to the beans, along with raisins. Turn it gently with a spoon before serving so that everything is mixed together and coated with the dressing.

Approx. preparation and cooking time: 1-1½ hours.

Red Kidney Bean Salad

225g (8 oz) red kidney beans or 2 × 425g (15 oz) cans
2 tbsp wine vinegar
1 tbsp tomato ketchup
4 tbsp olive oil
Sea salt; freshly ground black pepper
1 small onion, peeled and cut into thin rings
Chopped parsley

It is a good idea to make this salad in advance to give the beans a chance to soak up the flavour of the dressing.

Cover beans with cold water and leave to soak overnight; or for a quick soak, put into saucepan, cover with water, boil for 2 minutes and leave to soak for 1 hour. Then drain and rinse the beans. Put the beans into a saucepan, cover with water and boil vigorously for 10 minutes, then simmer gently for about 1 hour, until beans are tender. Drain. In a large bowl combine vinegar, ketchup, oil and seasoning; add drained beans and onion, and mix well. Cool. Sprinkle with chopped parsley.

Approx. preparation and cooking time (not including soaking): 1 hour 10 minutes.

Salade Niçoise with Butter Beans

2 tbsp chopped parsley
1 clove garlic, peeled and crushed
2 tbsp wine vinegar
6 tbsp olive oil
Sea salt; freshly ground black pepper
125g (4 oz) butter beans, soaked and cooked or
1 × 425g (15 oz) can
75-100g (3-4 oz) black olives
450g (1 lb) French beans, cooked
1 lettuce, washed and shaken dry
450g (1 lb) tomatoes, sliced

Put parsley, garlic, vinegar, oil, salt and pepper into a salad bowl and mix together. Drain butter beans and add, together with olives, French beans, lettuce and tomatoes. Turn salad over gently with a spoon until everything is well mixed and glossy with the dressing.

Serve with warm, crusty wholewheat bread.

Approx. preparation and cooking time (using ready-cooked beans): 10 minutes.

Black-eye Appetiser Salad

225g (8 oz) black-eye beans
2 stock cubes
Sea salt
1 small can artichoke hearts
9 tbsp French Dressing
1 small bunch radishes, finely sliced
2 sticks celery, finely chopped
6 spring onions, chopped
Sea salt; freshly ground black pepper
Lettuce

To garnish

Tomato quarters

Soak beans in ½L/1 pt water overnight. Drain beans and place in saucepan with ¾L/1¼ pts water, stock cubes and a little sea salt. Cook gently for 1-1½ hours or until tender. Drain and cool.

Cut artichoke hearts into bite-size pieces. Put in screw-top jar with French dressing and leave to marinate. Pour over drained beans then add radishes, celery and spring onions. Toss to mix, season to taste then pile onto lettuce-lined individual serving plates and garnish with tomato. Chill before serving.

Approx. preparation and cooking time (not including soaking): 1½ hours.

Lentil, Rice & Mushroom Salad

225g (8 oz) continental lentils
225g (8 oz) brown rice
12g (½ oz) vegetable margarine
100g (4 oz) mushrooms
8 spring onions
1 medium green pepper
1 tbsp finely chopped walnuts
15cm (6 in) piece of cucumber

Dressing

5 dsp vegetable oil
1 dsp cider vinegar
1 garlic clove
Sea salt; freshly ground black pepper

Put washed rice with double the amount of water in a pan, bring to boil then simmer for 30 minutes or until rice is soft and liquid absorbed. Cook lentils for 30-40 minutes until soft but not mushy.

Mix all dressing ingredients together. Drain lentils and mix with cooked rice. Place in salad bowl and toss in dressing. Just before serving, mix in nuts, onions, pepper, chopped cucumber and sliced raw mushrooms.

Approx. preparation and cooking time: 45 minutes.

Crunchy Salad

1 cupful sprouted chick peas
50g (2 oz) Red Leicester cheese
Handful fresh parsley

Cube cheese. Cut parsley roughly with scissors. Add to chickpeas with a little oil and vinegar, or yoghurt salad dressing.

Approx. preparation time: 5 minutes.

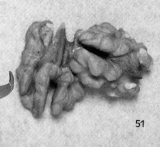

Russian Salad

100g (4 oz) cooked diced potatoes
100g (4 oz) haricot beans or dried peas (cooked)
100g (4 oz) cooked diced beetroot
2-3 tbsp French dressing
Chopped fresh parsley

Mix all ingredients together. Sprinkle chopped parsley over and chill for at least one hour before serving.

Approx. preparation time (not including chilling): 5 minutes.

Herby Haricot Bean Salad

Serves 4-6
6 tbsp olive oil
2 tbsp wine vinegar
1 tsp sugar
½ tsp mustard powder
1-2 garlic cloves, peeled and crushed (opt.)
Sea salt; freshly ground black pepper
225g (8 oz) dried haricot beans, soaked, cooked and drained
2 heaped tbsp chopped fresh herbs as available (parsley, chives, mint, tarragon, basil)

First make the dressing by putting the oil, vinegar, sugar, mustard and garlic into the base of a wooden salad bowl and mixing with a little sea salt and freshly ground black pepper. Add all the other ingredients and mix well so that everything is coated with the shiny dressing. If you add the beans while they are still warm, the salad will be all the better for it because they will absorb the dressing and flavourings so well.

This salad is best made an hour or so before it is required so that the beans have time to absorb the flavours of the herbs. Serve it well-chilled for lunch or supper with warm wholewheat bread and chilled white wine.

Approx. preparation time (using cooked beans): 5-10 minutes.

Dressings

☆ Avocado Dressing ☆

1 large ripe avocado
Juice of ½ lemon
1 tbsp wine or cider vinegar
1 tbsp cold-pressed olive oil
Sea salt; freshly ground black pepper

Halve, stone and skin avocado. Put flesh into blender or food processor with rest of ingredients. Whizz to a luscious pale green cream. A drop or two of tabasco sauce or a pinch or two of curry powder will enliven the flavour.

Approx. preparation time: 5 minutes.

Vinaigrette

2 tbsp wine vinegar, cider vinegar or lemon juice
1 tsp mustard powder
6 tbsp olive or sunflower oil
Freshly ground black pepper

Put everything into screwtop jar and shake together. Keep in fridge and use as needed.

Approx. preparation time: 5 minutes.

Yoghurt Dressing

150ml (5 fl oz) natural yoghurt
1-2 tbsp lemon juice
Chopped fresh herbs
Freshly ground black pepper

Just mix everything together.

Approx. preparation time: 5 minutes.

Tofu Dressing

150g (5 oz) tofu
2 tbsp wine or cider vinegar
1 tbsp cold-pressed olive oil
Chopped fresh herbs
Freshly ground black pepper

Put tofu into bowl and break up with fork, then beat in remaining ingredients. Or whizz everything together in a blender or food processor.

Approx. preparation time: 5 minutes.

Mayonnaise

2 free-range egg yolks
½ tsp dry mustard
½ tsp raw sugar
2 tbsp wine or cider vinegar
200ml (7 fl oz) cold-pressed sunflower oil
2 tbsp boiling water

Put egg yolks in blender or food processor with mustard, sugar and vinegar and whizz until well-blended. Then, with blender or food processor still running, gradually pour in oil, starting very slowly. Speed up once emulsion is formed and you hear the sound change to a 'glug-glug' noise. Finally, add the boiling water to thin and lighten the mixture. This will keep, covered, in the fridge for a week and makes about 200ml (8 fl oz).

Approx. preparation time: 10 minutes.

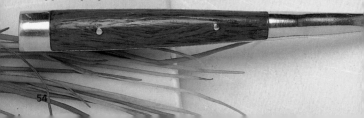

Tahini Mayonnaise

1 heaped tbsp tahini
2 tbsp cold water
1 tbsp lemon juice
1 garlic clove, crushed (opt.)
Sea salt; freshly ground black pepper

Put tahini in a bowl and gradually beat in water and lemon juice; mixture will form an emulsion, like normal mayonnaise. Add garlic, if using, and season to taste. Chopped herbs can be added too. Use as ordinary mayonnaise.

Approx. preparation time: 5 minutes.

Cottage Cheese Dressing

225g (8 oz) carton cottage cheese
150ml (¼ pt) single cream or top of the milk

Liquidize together the cottage cheese and single cream or top of the milk. Serve poured over almost any salad to provide a delicious, not-too-fattening creamy dressing and plenty of protein.

Approx. preparation time: 3-5 minutes.

Variations

Cottage cheese and chive dressing
Make as above, adding 1-2 tbsp of finely chopped chives or the green part of spring onions.

Cottage cheese and cucumber dressing
Add ¼ cucumber and 2 sprigs of mint to the Cottage Cheese Dressing and liquidize.

Main Courses
and Sauces

The Main Course recipes are divided into dishes which are heated through on top of the cooker or under the grill and those which favour long, slow cooking in the oven. Some of the cooker-top dishes can be transferred to the oven to finish cooking if you wish to take up spare oven space.

Some dishes automatically contain complementary protein, others can be boosted to make an even more nourishing meal with brown rice, wholewheat bread or yoghurt.

Cooker-top and Grill

Cooked pulses make excellent cutlets, rissoles and burgers — just taste Lentil Rissoles, crispy outside and moist within, with a piquant sauce or try them for a change with an icy-cold yoghurt dressing. Remember that pulses intended for cutlets, rissoles and burgers should not be reduced to a *very* soft consistency. Cook split peas and red lentils in just enough liquid to be absorbed during cooking time: 50ml (2 fl oz) to every 25g (1 oz) unsoaked pulses and half that amount for soaked ones. Split red lentils can also be steamed if that is easier. Drain other pulses well after cooking and chill mix for easier working.

You can save time with a pressure cooker or dry grind the harder beans if they are to be used for rissoles, cutlets, burgers and similar dishes.

Lentil Cutlets

175g (6 oz) continental lentils
1 large onion
1 clove garlic
2 hardboiled eggs
Chopped parsley
50g (2 oz) wholemeal breadcrumbs
1 egg yolk
Mace; sea salt; freshly ground black pepper
Wholewheat flour
Vegetable oil

Soak, cook and drain lentils. Peel and finely chop onion then sauté with crushed garlic for 10 minutes. Remove from heat, add chopped hardboiled eggs with rest of ingredients and cooked lentils. Stir well and season to taste. Leave to cool, then shape into half-inch thick cutlets. Coat with egg yolk and flour then fry in shallow oil for a couple of minutes each side until golden brown. Drain on kitchen paper and serve with barbeque style tomato sauce.

Approx. preparation and cooking time (not including soaking): 50 minutes.

⭐ Butter Beans with Apricots, ⭐ Cinnamon and Almonds

Serves 2-3 as a main dish
1 onion, chopped
2 tbsp oil
1½-2 tsp cinnamon
125g (4 oz) butter beans, cooked and drained
125g (4 oz) dried apricots, sliced
40g (1½ oz) raisins
400ml (¾ pt) water
25g (1 oz) creamed coconut
1 tbsp lemon juice
Sea salt; freshly ground black pepper
50g (2 oz) toasted flaked almonds ·

Fry onion in oil in a large saucepan for 10 minutes then stir in cinnamon and cook for a minute or two. Add beans, apricots, raisins and water, bring to the boil then turn heat down and leave to simmer, covered, for 15-20 minutes, until apricots are tender. Add coconut cream, lemon juice and seasoning. Sprinkle almonds on top before serving with fluffy long grain brown rice and a green salad.

Approx. preparation and cooking time:

Spicy Continental Lentil Rissoles

225g (8 oz) continental lentils
275ml (½ pt) water
2 tbsp oil
1 large onion, peeled and chopped
1 large clove garlic, crushed
1 small green pepper, de-seeded and chopped
1 tsp turmeric
1 tsp ground coriander
1 tsp ground cumin
¼-½ tsp chilli powder
Sea salt; freshly ground black pepper

To finish:

1 egg, beaten with 1 tbsp water
Dried crumbs
Oil for shallow frying

Wash and soak lentils as usual, then rinse and put into saucepan with the water. Simmer gently until tender and all liquid is absorbed, 30-45 minutes.

Meanwhile heat oil in a medium-sized saucepan and fry onion for 5 minutes or so, then add garlic and green pepper and cook for further 5 minutes; stir in spices and let them cook for another minute or so. Add fried vegetables and spices to cooked lentils, season with salt and pepper, then leave mixture to get cold. Form into small rissoles and dip first into beaten egg then into dried crumbs. Fry rissoles in shallow oil until crisp on both sides then drain on kitchen paper.

Serve with buttery wholewheat noodles or brown rice and curry or tomato sauce. Also good cold with natural yoghurt, mango chutney and salad.

Approx. preparation and cooking time (not including soaking): 1 hour.

Spiced Soya Rissoles

225g (8 oz) soya beans, soaked overnight
1 medium onion
2 cloves garlic
1cm (½ inch) cube root ginger
1 tbsp water
1 tsp oil
1 tsp ground cumin seeds
1 tsp ground coriander
½ tsp turmeric
Pinch cayenne pepper
Juice ½ lemon
Little beaten free-range egg
3 tbsp wholewheat flour
Oil for frying

Drain soya beans and cook in boiling water for 2½-3 hours until soft (or pressure cook at 15 lb pressure for 30 minutes). Drain and mash. Chop onion and garlic, grate ginger. Place in liquidizer with the water and blend until smooth. Fry this in tsp of oil until dry, then stir in rest of spices. Add mashed beans and stir over heat until well-blended. Remove from heat, add lemon juice and sufficient egg to make a moist consistency that will hold together. Shape into 4 flat rounds and coat with flour. Chill for 30 minutes until firm. Fry rissoles in oil for 5 minutes each side until outside is golden brown. Drain and serve with crisp green salad and a lightly spiced rice dish to balance the protein. Also good cold.

Approx. preparation and cooking time (not including soaking) and chilling): 3½ hours.

Split Pea Cutlets
with Apple Rings

350g (12 oz) yellow split peas
400ml (¾ pt) water
1 large onion, peeled and chopped
25g (1 oz) butter
½ tsp sage
Pinch ground cloves
1 egg
Sea salt; freshly ground black pepper
A little lemon juice

To finish:

Wholewheat flour
1 egg, beaten with 1 tbsp water
Dry crumbs
Oil for shallow frying

For Apple Rings:

2 medium-sized cooking apples
25g (1 oz) butter
2 tbsp oil

Soak split peas in water, then rinse. Put them in a saucepan with the water and cook until tender; drain if necessary and dry by stirring over a moderate heat for a minute or two.

Fry onion in butter in a large saucepan for 10 minutes, then add sage, split peas, ground cloves and egg. Mix well, mashing split peas a bit with the spoon then season with salt and pepper, adding a little lemon juice if required.

Shape split pea mixture into 12 small cutlets on a floured board, then dip each in egg and dry crumbs, coating well. Fry cutlets in shallow oil until crisp on both sides; drain on kitchen paper and keep warm.

To make apple rings, peel apples and remove cores with an apple corer, keeping apples whole. Slice into thin rings. Heat butter and oil in a clean frying-pan and fry apple rings for a minute or two each side to cook through and brown lightly. Serve the cutlets with the apple rings.

Approx. preparation and cooking time (not including soaking): 50 minutes.

Adzuki Bean, Carrot and Ginger Stir-fry

1 onion, sliced
4 tbsp oil
700g (1½ lbs) carrots, thinly sliced
1 tbsp grated fresh ginger
125g (4 oz) adzuki beans, soaked, cooked and drained
300ml (½ pt) water or stock
Bunch spring onions, chopped
Sea salt; freshly ground black pepper
Sugar

Fry onion in a large saucepan for 4-5 minutes until beginning to soften, then add carrots and ginger and stir-fry for a further 3-4 minutes. Add the adzuki beans and water, cover and leave to simmer gently for 10-15 minutes, until carrots are just tender. Stir in spring onions. Season with salt and pepper and a dash of sugar if necessary.

Serve with fluffy long grain brown rice and a side salad.

Approx. preparation and cooking time (using cooked beans): 25-30 minutes.

Beans Italian Style

450g (1 lb) pinto beans
4 tbsp vegetable oil
2 sage leaves or 2 tsp dried sage
2 tbsp tomato purée
1 onion
2 cloves garlic
Sea salt; freshly ground black pepper

Soak beans and cook for 1-1¼ hours. Drain and rinse. Heat oil and sauté onion with garlic for 5 minutes. Chop sage leaves and add to pan with the beans. Cook until fat is absorbed, then add tomato purée and season well. Serve with vegetables or brown rice and salad.

Approx. preparation and cooking time (not including soaking): 1½-1¾ hours.

Chilli Beans with Coconut

225g (8 oz) red kidney beans
1 medium onion
1 clove garlic
1 tbsp vegetable oil
½ tsp chilli powder
½L/1 pt vegetable stock
25g (1 oz) creamed coconut
Sea salt

Wash and soak beans, then rinse, drain and soak once more. Fry chopped onion and crushed garlic clove in oil until soft and golden. Add chilli powder, then sauté a few more minutes, stirring frequently. Pour in stock. Drain beans and add to pan. Bring to boil and simmer for 5 minutes.

Warm a wide-necked vacuum jar and spoon in the beans with enough stock to fill the jar and leave a small space at the top. Close and leave for 6 hours or overnight.

Pour beans into pan, bring back to boil and simmer for 20 minutes or until quite soft. Break up creamed coconut with a fork and mix to cream with a little of liquid from pan. Stir into bean mixture and add sea salt to taste.

Approx. preparation and cooking time (not including soaking and overnight cooking): 35 minutes.

Butter Beans with Mushrooms in Creamy Sauce

1 tbsp sunflower oil
1 large onion, peeled and chopped
225g (8 oz) small white button mushrooms
100g (4 oz) butter beans, soaked, rinsed and cooked for at least 1 hour until tender or 1×425g (15 oz) can
150ml (6 oz) fromage blanc
½ tsp paprika pepper
Sea salt; freshly ground black pepper
Chopped parsley

Heat oil in a medium-sized saucepan and fry onion for about 7 minutes until nearly soft but not brown. While onion is cooking, wash and slice mushrooms then add to saucepan with butter beans and cook for about 5 minutes until mushrooms are tender and beans heated through. Stir often. Add fromage blanc and bring just up to the boil, stirring all the time. Take off heat, add paprika, salt and pepper to taste and serve immediately, sprinkled with chopped parsley. The mixture shouldn't get too hot after fromage blanc is added or it will curdle a little, although still taste all right. Serve with plainly cooked brown rice and a crisp green salad.

Approx. preparation and cooking time (using cooked beans): 15 minutes.

Spiced Lentils with Rice

175g (6 oz) brown lentils
700ml (1¼ pt) water
1 bay leaf
1 tbsp oil
1 onion, peeled and chopped
1 green or red pepper, de-seeded and sliced
1 garlic clove, peeled and crushed
175g (6 oz) button mushrooms, washed
2 tomatoes, washed and sliced
1 tsp curry powder
1 tsp ground coriander
1 tbsp lemon juice
1 tbsp tomato paste
Sea salt; freshly ground black pepper

Put lentils, water and bay leaf into medium-sized saucepan and simmer gently for 45-60 minutes until lentils are very tender. Remove bay leaf. Heat oil in a large saucepan and fry the onion for 5 minutes until beginning to soften, then add pepper, garlic, mushrooms, tomatoes and lentils and fry for a further 2-3 minutes. Add the spices, lemon juice and tomato paste and cook gently for a further 4-5 minutes, until everything is heated through. Check seasoning and serve, garnished with the raw onion rings and remaining tomato. This can be served hot with a side salad or cold as a protein salad in a border of watercress and sliced tomato with warm wholewheat bread.

Approx. preparation and cooking time: 1 hour 10 minutes.

Bean Paella

125g (4 oz) red kidney beans (or a mixture)
1 small aubergine, diced
225g (8 oz) long grain brown rice
400ml (¾ pt) water
½ tsp turmeric
2 tbsp oil
1 large onion, peeled and chopped
1 green pepper, de-seeded and chopped
1 stick celery, chopped
2 large carrots, scraped and diced
1 large clove garlic, crushed
2 large tomatoes, peeled and chopped (or use canned ones)
125g (4 oz) button mushrooms, wiped and sliced
Sea salt; freshly ground black pepper
2 tbsp chopped parsley

Wash, soak and rinse beans, then cook until tender and drain. Sprinkle aubergine with sea salt and leave for 30 minutes to draw out bitter juices, then rinse and pat dry on kitchen paper. Meanwhile, wash rice and put into large saucepan with the water, turmeric and sea salt. Bring to the boil, stir, put lid on saucepan and reduce heat. Let rice cook gently for 30 minutes.

Heat oil in a saucepan and fry prepared onion, pepper, celery, carrots, aubergine and garlic for 10 minutes without browning, then add tomatoes and mushrooms and cook for 5 minutes more. Tip this mixture on top of the rice, add beans, then put lid on saucepan and cook over low heat for a further 15 minutes. Turn off heat and leave paella to stand for another 10 minutes. Then stir mixture carefully with fork, season to taste and add chopped parsley. Reheat gently if necessary before serving.

Approx. preparation and cooking time (not including soaking): 1½ hours.

Spicy Lentil Burgers

450g (1 lb) continental lentils
¾L (1½ pts) hot water
100g (4 oz) vegetable margarine
2 onions, finely chopped
1 medium green pepper, finely chopped
2 carrots, finely chopped
1 fresh chilli
1 tsp mixed herbs
½ tsp powdered mace
1 tsp cayenne pepper
4 tsp tomato purée
2 cloves garlic
Sea salt; freshly ground black pepper

Wash lentils, put in pan with the water and bring to the boil. Cover and simmer gently for 1 hour or until lentils are mushy and have absorbed all the liquid. The lentils should be very well cooked to form into burgers more easily.

Sauté chopped onion, carrot and crushed garlic in margarine for 5 minutes. Add chopped pepper and chilli and fry gently for a further 5 minutes. Season and mash lentils, then mix in vegetables, herbs, spices and tomato purée. Shape into approx. 24 small rounds, dust with wholewheat flour and fry gently on both sides until brown.

Approx. preparation and cooking time: 1½ hours.

67

Curried Soya Beans

225g (8 oz) dried soya beans
2 tbsp vegetable oil
1 large onion, chopped
1 clove garlic, crushed
2.5cm (1-inch) piece root ginger, sliced
1 green chilli, deseeded and chopped
1 tsp turmeric
2 tsp ground coriander
1 tsp ground cumin
½ tsp chilli powder
1 tsp paprika
Sea salt

Soak dried beans in ½L (1 pt) cold water overnight. Drain, reserving water, and put in saucepan. Add sufficient water to bring soaking water up to 1L (2 pts) and pour over beans. Cover pan and bring to boil. Reduce heat and simmer for 2-3 hours or until beans are tender. Drain and reserve cooking stock.

Meanwhile, heat oil in a saucepan, add onion and garlic and fry for 3 minutes, stirring frequently. Add ginger and chilli and cook for 3 minutes more. Mix turmeric, coriander, cumin and paprika together, adding enough cold water to make a paste. Add to onion mixture and fry, stirring constantly for 5 minutes. (Add a little bean stock if mixture is too dry.) Pour in ½L (1 pt) bean stock gradually, mixing well. Season with salt, bring to boil, add the soya beans. Cover pan and simmer for 1 hour or cook, covered, in the oven at 350°F (180°C), gas mark 4 for 1 hour. Serve on a bed of brown rice garnished with toasted almonds.

Approx. preparation and cooking time (not including soaking): 4 hours.

Bengal Black-eye Beans

225g (8 oz) black-eye beans (soaked overnight)
2 onions, finely chopped
1 green chilli, finely chopped
2.5cm (1-inch) piece fresh ginger, grated
2 black cardamoms
6 black peppercorns
2.5cm (1-inch) piece cinnamon stick
6 cloves
4 cloves garlic, finely chopped
½ tsp paprika
1 tsp turmeric
½ tsp ground cumin
2 tsp ground coriander
1 tbsp fresh coriander leaves, finely chopped
1 tsp garam masala
3 tbsp lemon juice

Put beans in saucepan with half the onion and the following
six ingredients. Cover with cold water, bring to boil and simmer
until tender — about 50 minutes. Drain and keep the stock.
Place oil in a pan and cook onion and garlic for 2 minutes. Add
paprika, turmeric, cumin and coriander, stirring well. Add
drained beans and stir gently. Mix in coriander leaves, garam
masala and lemon juice then add sufficient stock to make sauce,
simmering gently. Serve with brown rice.

**Approx. preparation and cooking time (not including
soaking): 1 hour.**

Felafel

225g (8 oz) chick peas
1 large onion
1 tsp ground coriander
1 tsp ground cumin
Large pinch chilli powder
1 clove garlic, crushed
Sea salt; freshly ground black pepper

To finish:

Wholewheat flour to coat
Vegetable oil for shallow frying

Soak chick peas in cold water for several hours, then drain, cover with fresh cold water and simmer gently until very tender (1-2 hours). Drain the chick peas and pass them through a fairly fine blade on a vegetable mill.

Peel and finely grate the onion and add it to the chick peas, together with the spices, garlic and sea salt and freshly ground black pepper to taste. If the mixture is rather soft, place in the fridge for about 30 minutes to firm up.

Form tablespoonfuls of the mixture into small, flat cakes, coat them well with wholewheat flour, then shallow fry in hot oil until brown on both sides.

Split peas can be used instead of chick peas — as these cook to a soft mush they can be mashed rather than milled but only use as much water as they will absorb during cooking or they will be too moist.

Serve with pitta bread or accompanied by seasonal vegetables and garnished with lemon and parsley.

Approx. preparation and cooking time (not including soaking): 2 hours 20 minutes.

Lentil Shepherd's Pie

1 large onion
1 stick celery
1 tbsp oil
175g (6 oz) red lentils
450ml (¾ pt) vegetable stock
½ tsp yeast extract
Pinch thyme and dried sage
175g (6 oz) carrots, finely grated

Topping:

450g (1 lb) potatoes
Bay leaf
Knob unsalted butter or soft vegetable margarine
Skim milk
Freshly ground black pepper

Finely chop onion and celery and cook gently in oil for 2 minutes. Add lentils, stock, yeast extract, thyme, sage, and grated carrots and simmer for 30 minutes. Scrub potatoes and cut into 5cm (2-inch) pieces. Place in pan with bay leaf and cover with water. Bring to the boil, then simmer for 20-25 minutes until soft. Drain, reserving fluid for stock, remove bay leaf and mash with butter or margarine and enough milk to give a soft creamy consistency. Season.

Place lentil mixture in base of a heatproof dish, cover with potato. Place under grill for 5 minutes or until crispy and golden.

Serve hot with a green vegetable.

Approx. preparation and cooking time: 40 minutes.

Oven Bakes

Loaves, casseroles, pies and other bakes — again, versatile beans and pulses can be used to make meals to suit every occasion and appetite. Although some oven-baked dishes take a long time to cook, they are often quick and easy to prepare and make an ideal dish to put on to cook while out shopping, cheering the school team or otherwise busily engaged, so that you and the family can return to a piping hot, perfectly-cooked meal — a real boon on a cold wintry day.

Lentils and beans can be used to make excellent loaves and they can be cooked in the oven alongside roast or baked potatoes and served with lightly-cooked vegetables and a brown gravy-type sauce or serve hot or cold sliced with salads for a summer lunch or supper. Remember that combining pulses with rice, pasta or with pastry in a pie has the effect of joining complementary proteins to make first-class or complete proteins and a very satisfying meal.

For really speedy meals, make use of canned red kidney beans, chick peas and others as available.

⭐ Butter Bean and Chutney Roll ⭐

150g (6 oz) wholewheat flour
1 slightly rounded tsp baking powder
Sea salt
75g (3 oz) polyunsaturated margarine
1 tbsp water
2 large onions, peeled and thinly sliced
1 tbsp oil
100g (3-4 oz) butter beans, soaked, rinsed and cooked, or 1×425g (15 oz) can
2 rounded tbsp sweet chutney — mango or sugar-free type
1 tsp dried basil
Freshly ground black pepper
Milk or beaten egg for glazing (opt.)

Make pastry: Sift flour, baking powder and pinch of salt into bowl, adding residue of bran in sieve. Mix in soft margarine using a fork. When mixture resembles coarse breadcrumbs, add water and mix to a dough. Leave to rest while making filling.

Set oven to 400°F (200°C), gas mark 6. Fry onion in oil for about 10 minutes until soft, stirring to prevent sticking. Drain butter beans and mix them with onion, chutney, basil, and season with salt and pepper.

Roll out pastry to oval about 30×25cm (12×10 inches) and spoon butter bean mixture onto centre. Brush edges of pastry with a little cold water and bring sides of pastry up to centre, pressing together and making an attractive join to resemble large Cornish pasty. Brush with a little milk or beaten egg if wished then bake roll for 30-35 minutes until golden brown. Serve with a green vegetable, mashed potatoes and a savoury sauce.

Approx. preparation and cooking time (using cooked beans): 1 hour.

Lazy Lentils

4 large onions, peeled and chopped
1 tbsp olive oil
1 garlic clove, crushed
250ml (½ pt) water
2 tsp yeast extract
175g (6 oz) split red lentils
1 tsp mixed herbs
Sea salt; freshly ground black pepper
125g (4 oz) grated cheese
Breadcrumbs

Set oven to 300°F (150°C), gas mark 3. (If pre-setting it, time it for 2 hours.) Using a flameproof casserole if possible, fry onions in butter for 5-7 minutes, browning lightly, then add garlic, water and yeast extract and stir until extract has dissolved. Take off heat, add lentils, herbs, seasoning and most of cheese. Sprinkle rest of cheese on top together with some crumbs, then bake for 2 hours. Serve with vegetables and gravy or a parsley sauce.

Approx. preparation and cooking time: 2¼ hours.

Red Bean Lasagne

Serves 6
150g (6 oz) wholewheat lasagne
Sea salt
1 large onion, peeled and chopped
1 tbsp oil
150g (6 oz) red kidney beans, soaked, cooked for 1-1¼ hours until tender or use 2 tins red kidney beans
225g (8 oz) can tomatoes
2 tbsp tomato paste
1 tsp powdered cinnamon
Freshly ground black pepper; dash of honey

Cheese Sauce & Topping

25g (1 oz) polyunsaturated margarine
50g (2 oz) flour
575ml (1 pt) skimmed milk
125g (4 oz) strongly-flavoured cheese, grated

Half-fill large saucepan with water, add 1 tsp salt. Bring to boil then put in lasagne, easing in gently as it softens in water. Boil without lid for about 10 minutes, until tender. Drain lasagne and drape the pieces over sides of saucepan to prevent them sticking together while filling is prepared.

Fry onion in oil in a medium saucepan for 10 minutes, until tender. Drain beans, keeping liquid. Add beans to onions, mashing a little to break up, also add tomatoes, tomato paste, cinnamon, salt, pepper and a dash of honey if needed.

Make low-fat cheese sauce by putting margarine, flour and milk into liquidizer goblet and blending, then transfer to saucepan and stir over moderate heat until thickened. Or make in usual way by melting fat in saucepan, stirring in flour then adding milk and stirring over heat until thickened. Stir in half cheese and season to taste.

Set oven to 400°F (200°C), gas mark 6. Put layer of bean mixture into shallow ovenproof dish and cover with some lasagne. Follow with another layer of bean mixture then more lasagne and any remaining beans. Pour cheese sauce over top and sprinkle with rest of cheese. Bake for about 45 minutes until golden and bubbling.

Serve with simply-cooked green vegetable or a crisp green salad such as a combination of watercress, celery and lettuce.

Approx. preparation and cooking time (using cooked beans): 1¼ hours.

Lentil Lasagne

175g (6 oz) wholewheat lasagne
1 onion, peeled and chopped
1 tbsp oil
125g (4 oz) mushrooms, wiped and chopped
425g (15 oz) can tomatoes
125g (4 oz) split red lentils
150ml (¼ pt) stock or red wine
3 large garlic cloves, peeled and crushed
½ tsp each dried basil, thyme, oregano, marjoram
Sea salt; freshly ground black pepper
225g (8 oz) cottage cheese
125g (4 oz) grated Cheddar cheese
A few wholewheat breadcrumbs; a little Parmesan cheese

Cook lasagne in a large saucepan, half-filled with boiling salted water; drain and drape lasagne over sides of colander so they don't stick together while you prepare filling. Fry onion in oil for 7 minutes, add mushrooms and cook for further 3 minutes, then stir in tomatoes, lentils, water or wine and crushed garlic. Cook gently for 20-30 minutes until lentils are very tender. Add herbs and season to taste. Set oven to 400°F (200°C), gas mark 6.

Put a layer of the lentil mixture in the base of a lightly-greased shallow casserole dish. Cover with some lasagne, followed by another layer of lentils, some cottage cheese, some grated cheese then lasagne. Continue in layers until everything is used. Sprinkle top with some crumbs and grated Parmesan cheese and bake in oven for 1 hour. Serve hot with salad.

Approx. preparation and cooking time: 1½ hours

Pease Pudding

225g (8 oz) yellow split peas
1 large onion, chopped
50g (2 oz) butter
1 egg
Sea salt; freshly ground black pepper

Cook split peas in plenty of water until tender, then drain.
Meanwhile fry onion in butter for 10 minutes. Add onion to
peas then beat in egg and season to taste. Turn mixture into
a buttered bowl, cover with foil and steam for one hour or bake
the mixture in a greased casserole dish in a moderate oven
350°F (180°C), gas mark 4 for 30-40 minutes.

Serve with jacket-baked potatoes, mint sauce and a green
vegetable.

Approx. preparation and cooking time: 1-1½ hours.

Haricot Bean Flan

125g (4 oz) wholewheat shortcrust pastry
1 onion, chopped
125g (4 oz) haricot beans, soaked and cooked
25g (1 oz) butter
125g (4 oz) strongly-flavoured Cheddar cheese
1 egg
150ml (¼ pt) creamy milk
1 tsp dry mustard
Sea salt; freshly ground black pepper
2 tomatoes, sliced

Set oven to 400°F (200°C), gas mark 6. Roll out pastry and line a 20cm (8-inch) flan tin. Prick base and bake for 15-20 minutes. Fry onion in butter for 10 minutes then pour into hot flan case. Reduce oven setting to 350°F (180°C), gas mark 4. Drain beans thoroughly. Arrange beans and cheese evenly in flan. Whisk together egg, milk, mustard and seasoning. Pour into flan then arrange tomato slices on top. Bake for 35-40 minutes, until set.

Serve with crisp salad or lightly-cooked vegetables.

Approx. preparation and cooking time (using cooked beans): 1 hour 10 minutes.

Lentil and Cheese Slice

225g (8 oz) split red lentils
1 onion, sliced
1 bay leaf
450ml (16 fl oz) water
50g (2 oz) grated cheese
Sea salt; freshly ground black pepper
1 tomato, thinly sliced
A little soft margarine

Put lentils, onion and bay leaf into saucepan with the water and cook gently without a lid for 20-25 minutes, until lentils are tender. Remove bay leaf. Set oven to 425°F (220°C), gas mark 7. Beat half the cheese into the cooked lentils and season. Grease a 20cm (8-inch) square tin, spoon in lentil mixture, spreading to corners. Top with remaining cheese and tomato slices, dot with margarine. Bake for 20-25 minutes.

Serve with parsley sauce, new potatoes and a green vegetable. Also good cold with salad.

Approx. preparation and cooking time: 55 minutes.

Continental Lentil and Walnut Loaf

175g (6 oz) continental lentils
1 onion, peeled and chopped finely
1 large garlic clove, crushed
2 tbsp oil
1 tsp dried thyme
125g (4 oz) walnuts, ground or pulverized in liquidizer
125g (4 oz) wholewheat breadcrumbs
1 tbsp tomato purée
1 tbsp chopped fresh parsley
1 egg
Sea salt; freshly ground black pepper

To serve:

1 tomato, sliced
A few sprigs of parsley

Soak lentils for a few hours, then rinse and put into a saucepan with enough cold water to cover. Simmer gently for about 40 minutes until tender, then drain off any liquid.

Prepare a 450g (1 lb) loaf tin by putting a long strip of foil across the bottom and up the 2 narrow sides; grease generously with butter or margarine. Set oven to 375°F (190°C), gas mark 5.

Fry onion and garlic in the oil in a good-sized saucepan for 10 minutes until tender and lightly browned. Stir in thyme and cook for a few seconds then remove saucepan from heat and add lentils, walnuts, wholewheat breadcrumbs, tomato purée, parsley and egg. Mix well then season with salt and pepper. Spoon mixture into prepared loaf tin and smooth top. Cover with piece of greased foil and bake in oven for 1 hour. Leave in tin for a minute or two, then slip knife round edges of loaf to loosen it and turn it out, stripping off foil. Garnish top of loaf with slices of tomato and a sprig of parsley.

Serve hot with roast or baked potatoes, gravy and vegetables as a vegetarian-style Sunday lunch or cold with mayonnaise or chutney.

Approx. preparation and cooking time (not including soaking): 1 hour 45 minutes.

Soya Loaf

175g (6 oz) soya beans
1 large onion, peeled and chopped
2 cloves garlic, crushed
4 sticks celery, washed and chopped
20g (2 oz) butter
2 tomatoes, peeled and chopped
2 tbsp tomato purée
125g (4 oz) wholewheat breadcrumbs
4 tbsp chopped parsley
1 tsp dried thyme
1 egg
Sea salt; freshly ground black pepper

To finish:

A little butter
Dry crumbs

Soak, rinse and cook soya beans as usual (they will take about 4 hours to get really soft). Then drain and mash. Preheat oven to 375°F (190°C), gas mark 5.

Fry onion, garlic and celery in the butter in a good-sized saucepan for about 15 minutes until tender, then add tomatoes, tomato purée, and cook gently for a further 5 minutes. Stir in soya beans, wholewheat breadcrumbs, parsley, thyme and egg and season mixture with salt and pepper.

Grease a 450g (1 lb) loaf tin well with butter then coat with dried crumbs which should stick to the butter, helping loaf to come out of the tin easily and make the outside nice and crisp. Spoon soya mixture into tin and smooth down top. Cover with piece of buttered foil and bake in the oven for 1 hour. Let loaf stand for a minute or so then slip knife round edges and turn out onto warm dish. Serve with roast or baked potatoes, gravy and vegetables. Apple sauce goes well with it, too.

Approx. preparation and cooking time (not including soaking): 5 hours.

Vegetable and Bean Country Pie

75g (3 oz) adzuki beans
75g (3 oz) chick peas
75g (3 oz) red kidney beans
2 medium onions
2 carrots
Large wedge of swede or turnip
1 tsp cornflour
1 tbsp tamari sauce
150g (6 oz) wholewheat flour
75g (3 oz) margarine

Soak beans and cook 45 minutes or until tender. Cook adzuki beans separately so that other beans keep their colour. Drain well. Sauté onion in oil and mix in chopped carrots and other vegetables. Stir in the beans and add tamari sauce. Let mixture simmer for 20 minutes. Roll out pastry made from flour and margarine to fit pie plate. Pour in mixture and trim pastry edges. Bake in a moderately hot oven at 400°F (200°C), gas mark 6 for 25-30 minutes until golden brown.

Approx. preparation and cooking time (not including soaking): 1½ hours.

Lentil and Cider Loaf

Serves 6-8

175g (6 oz) split red lentils

400ml (¾ pt) cider

Butter and dried breadcrumbs for lining loaf tin

1 large onion, peeled and chopped

1 carrot (about 50g/2 oz), scraped and chopped

1 stick of celery, chopped

1 garlic clove, peeled and crushed

25g (1 oz) butter

1 tsp dried thyme

50g (2 oz) hazel nuts, roasted for 20 minutes in moderate oven until golden beneath skins, then ground in a liquidizer

50g (2 oz) cheese, grated

1 tbsp fresh parsley, chopped

1 egg

Sea salt; freshly ground black pepper

Parsley sprigs to decorate

Put lentils and cider into saucepan and bring to the boil; reduce heat, half-cover saucepan and leave to simmer over fairly low heat for 20 minutes until lentils are tender and all the water absorbed.

When lentils are nearly cooked, set oven to 350°F (180°C), gas mark 4. Prepare a 450g (1 lb) loaf tin by lining the base and narrow sides with a long strip of silicon paper; brush well with butter and sprinkle lightly with dried breadcrumbs. Next fry onion, carrot, celery and garlic in butter for 10 minutes, until softened and lightly browned. Add fried vegetables to the lentils, together with the thyme, nuts, cheese, parsley and egg. Mix together well and season to taste.

Spoon mixture into prepared tin, smooth over surface and cover with a piece of foil. Bake loaf in pre-heated oven for 1 hour, then remove foil and cook for a further 10-15 minutes, uncovered if necessary, to brown the top. To serve, slip a knife round the sides of the loaf and turn out onto warm dish. Decorate top with sprigs of fresh green parsley.

Approx. preparation and cooking time: 1¾ hours.

Boston Baked Beans

325g (12 oz) haricot beans
1 large onion
1 tbsp vegetable oil
1 tsp dry mustard
2 tsp molasses
200ml (⅓ pt) vegetable stock or water
150ml (¼ pt) tomato juice

Soak, drain and rinse beans. Cook until nearly tender and drain. Heat oven to 300°F (150°C), gas mark 2.

Sauté onion in oil for a few minutes, add all other ingredients and bring to the boil. Transfer to casserole and bake for about 4 hours, stirring occasionally and checking that beans are not too dry.

Serve with wholewheat toast, herb or garlic bread.

Approx. preparation and cooking time (not including soaking): 5½ hours.

Butter Bean and Cider Casserole ✓

15g (½ oz) butter or margarine
1 tbsp oil
3 large onions, peeled and sliced
2 garlic cloves, peeled and crushed
450g (1 lb) carrots, scraped and sliced
225g (8 oz) dried butter beans, soaked, cooked and drained or 2 × 425g (15 oz) cans, drained
275ml (½ pt) stock
150ml (¼ pt) cider
Bouquet garni
Sea salt; freshly ground black pepper

Set oven to 325°F (160°C), gas mark 3. Heat butter or margarine and oil in a large saucepan, add onions and garlic, fry for 5 minutes browning slightly, then stir in carrots and cook for 4-5 minutes more, stirring frequently to prevent sticking. Add butter beans, stock, cider, bouquet garni and a little salt and pepper. Bring to the boil, cover and transfer to oven for 1½-2 hours. If a slightly thicker gravy is preferred, stir in a teaspoon of cornflour or arrowroot blended with a little stock and let the mixture boil for a minute or two to thicken. Remove bouquet garni before serving.

Serve with hot crusty wholewheat rolls or jacket-baked potatoes and grated cheese. Or add a medium-sized peeled potato per person to the pot with the butter beans and vegetables and cook together so that the potatoes soak up the flavours.

Approx. preparation and cooking time (using cooked beans): 2-2¼ hours.

Baked Black-eye Beans

225g (8 oz) black-eye beans
1 large onion
2 medium carrots
100g (4 oz) mushrooms
1 small green pepper
2 cloves garlic
2 tbsp vegetable oil
½ tsp thyme
1 tsp marjoram
400ml (¾ pt) water or vegetable stock
Sea salt; freshly ground black pepper
Wholewheat breadcrumbs
75g (3 oz) grated cheese

Preheat oven to 350°F (180°C), gas mark 4. Soak, drain and rinse beans. Sauté crushed garlic, chopped onion, carrots, sliced mushrooms and pepper for 10 minutes in the oil. Add beans, herbs and water. Simmer for 30-45 minutes until beans are tender.

Liquidize or pass mixture through vegetable mill, season to taste and place in greased, shallow pie dish. Sprinkle breadcrumbs and grated cheese over bean mixture and bake for 30 minutes until top is golden and crunchy.

Approx. preparation and cooking time (not including soaking): 2 hours.

Sauces

If you are weight- or fat-watching, you can just purée cooked vegetables to make a very acceptable low-calorie sauce, thinning them with a little skimmed milk, low fat soft cheese, tofu or yoghurt, or lemon juice if needed. Reduce the calories in milk-based sauces by using skimmed instead of whole milk, too.

The sauce suggestions which follow make delicious accompaniments to a variety of 'dry' dishes, like loaves, rissoles, cutlets and burgers, spicing them or adding contrasting flavour, texture and colour.

☆ Spicy Peanut Sauce ☆

1 onion, peeled and chopped
1 tbsp olive oil
1 tbsp peanut butter
125g (4 oz) roasted peanuts, chopped or grated
450g (1 lb) tomatoes, skinned and chopped
Freshly ground black pepper

Make sauce by frying onion in the oil for 10 minutes, then add peanut butter, peanuts and tomatoes. Season to taste. Nice served with hot cauliflower.

Approx. preparation and cooking time: 15 minutes.

Tomato Sauce

1 medium onion, peeled and chopped
1 tbsp oil
425g (15 oz) can tomatoes or 450g (1 lb) fresh
1-2 tsp tomato paste
Sea salt; freshly ground black pepper; a little honey
½ tsp paprika (opt.)

Fry onion in oil in a medium-sized saucepan for 10 minutes but do not brown. Add tomatoes and liquidize mixture, sieving afterwards if using fresh tomatoes. Add tomato paste, salt and pepper to taste and a little honey if necessary. The paprika makes a pleasant addition or 2-3 tbsp red wine.

Approx. preparation and cooking time: 15 minutes.

Quick Blender White Sauce

25g (1 oz) butter
25g (1 oz) flour
400ml (¾ pt) milk
Sea salt; freshly ground black pepper

Put butter, flour and milk into liquidizer goblet; add about ½ tsp sea salt and a good grinding of black pepper. Blend at high speed for a few seconds to break up the butter and mix everything together. (A few lumpy bits of butter don't matter.) Turn mixture into medium-sized saucepan and put over a moderate heat, stir the sauce until it has thickened then reduce heat and leave sauce to simmer gently for 15 minutes. This is especially important because there has been no initial cooking of the flour so time must be allowed for this to avoid raw 'floury' taste.

Approx. preparation and cooking time: 20 minutes.

Variations

Quick blender cheese sauce
Add 125g (4 oz) gratd cheese after sauce has cooked.

Quick blender parsley sauce
Put some sprigs of parsley into liquidizer with the other ingredients at the beginning of the process.

Brown Gravy

1 onion, peeled and chopped
2 tbsp oil
1 rounded tbsp flour
1 clove garlic, crushed
Bouquet garni
400ml (¾ pt) hot stock
Sea salt; freshly ground black pepper

Brown onion in the oil, then add the flour and continue cooking until that is nut-brown, too. Then add garlic, bouquet garni and stock and simmer gently without lid on saucepan to cook the flour and reduce sauce to a good consistency. Strain before serving; season with salt and pepper.

Approx. preparation and cooking time: 20-30 minutes.

Curry Sauce – English Style

1 onion, peeled and chopped
1 apple, peeled and chopped
2 tbsp oil
1 tbsp curry powder
25g (1 oz) flour
400ml (¾ pt) stock or water
1 tbsp tomato purée
Sea salt; freshly ground black pepper
Lemon juice

Fry onion and apple in the oil in a medium-size saucepan for 10 minutes without browning, then add curry powder and fry for 1-2 minutes more. Stir in flour and cook for 2 minutes, then remove pan from heat and mix in stock or water and tomato purée. Return to heat and bring to the boil, stirring all the time. Let sauce simmer gently for 15 minutes without lid on saucepan, season with salt and pepper and a squeeze of lemon juice if required. Serve sauce as it is or liquidize if smoother texture is preferred.

Approx. preparation and cooking time: 30-35 minutes.

Index to Recipes